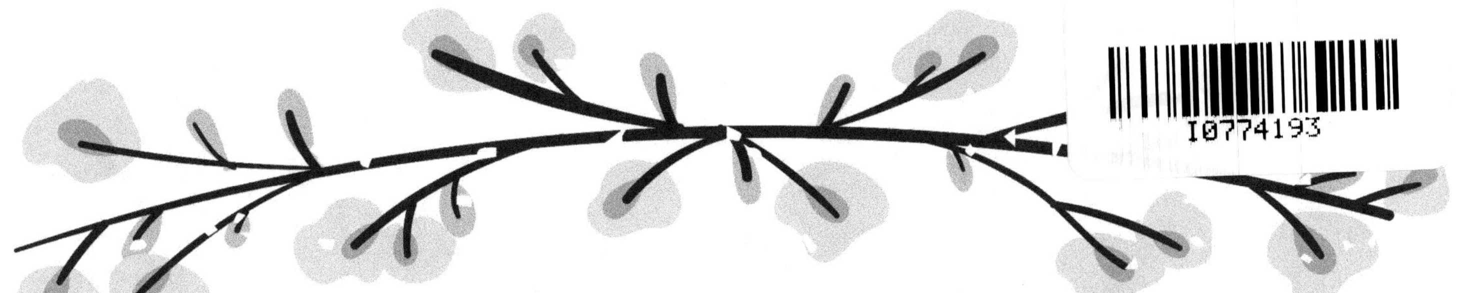

Philosophy for children

From child to children

Once upon a time!

God may you pay!

Coloring story!

By: Bernardo Octaviano Pereira

This book belongs to:

____

I dedicate this work, firstly, to my parents who I love so much, to my teachers, to my dear aunts and to all my friends, may God bless you all infinitely!

Bernardo Octaviano Pereira

17/04/2024

In a small town, not far from here, a man knocked on the door of a house looking for a glass of water.

The owner of the house, known for his avarice, gave in to the insistence of the visitor who was thirsty, and gave him a glass of water.

After drinking the water, the visitor thanked him with a simple "May God pay you". However, the owner of the house, with a mocking smile,

he replied that God was already burdened with debts, since everyone who owed something used to attribute the account to the name of God.

The visitor was surprised by the man's lack of respect for sacred words. He tried to explain that those words

They should not be used lightly as they were very heavy, but the owner of the house decided to test the weight of the words on the scales.

Then he wrote "God pay you" on a piece of paper and placed it on one pan of the scale, while on the other pan he placed a weight.

To his surprise, the plate with the paper tilted downwards, indicating that the words carried significant weight.

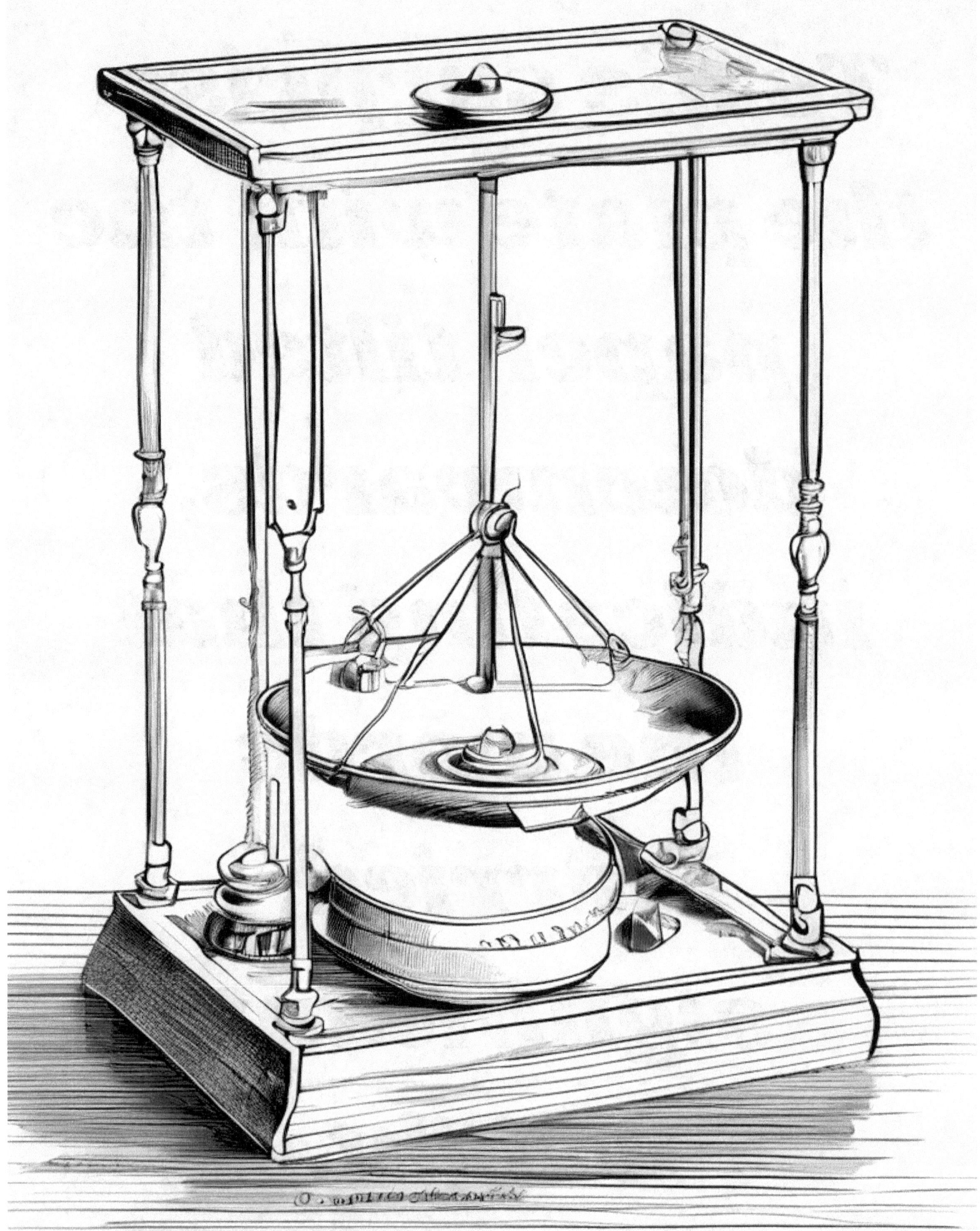

The man, determined to prove his point, added more weights to the opposite plate, but the scale remained unshakable.

No matter how hard he tried, the paper with the sacred words remained heavier than all the weights combined.

Finally, the owner of the house, with tears in his eyes, realized the true meaning behind that simple thank you.

He sincerely
apologized for
his foolish
behavior and
promised never
again to doubt
the power of
"Daddy in
Heaven's" words.

Since then, he learned to value every word that came out of the mouths of the humblest, especially those that carried the weight of gratitude and faith.

And so, he began to live a more generous and compassionate life, always aware of the power of words and the importance of honoring the divine in his actions and thoughts.

The end!

www.ingramcontent.com/pod-product-compliance
Lightning Source LLC
Chambersburg PA
CBHW081540250726
48659CB00009B/3020